ARMENIDA QYQJA

GOLDEN

ARMOR

Transcendent Zero Press
Houston, Texas

Cover art by Bruna Aliaj
Editorial assistance by Candice Louisa Daquin

Library of Congress Control Number: 2025933018

ISBN: 978-1-946460-62-2

GOLDEN ARMOR
ARMENIDA QYQJA

Indomitable Poetry of World Truth

Dustin Pickering

In the ancient myth of Pallas Athena, the goddess is born from Zeus through parthenogenesis. The goddess emerges from his forehead as full-grown. She becomes the goddess of war, one of indomitable spirit. An 1898 painting by Gustav Klimt presents her in golden armor to suggest the majesty of her divinity and power.

Golden Armor is a poetry collection about femininity, war, human rights abuses, and social concerns. Qyqja offers intriguing perspectives in the clarity of bold language. Most of the poems merge the female persona and her longings with contemporary concerns about global conflict and human initiative. Using a startling array of gentle symbolic images, *Golden Armor* is a remarkable act in literary citizenship.

In poems such as "Escalations of thoughts" Qyqja reminds the readers of the moment in front of them: "nothing is greater than / light itself and the actual being...." However, these poems do not shadow the global village immersed in war and genocide. Qyqja writes concerning the 1999 genocide in Kosovo, "your returned soul, century after century / doesn't

5

know why it is reborn, / drenched in blood again and again to die...." The feeling of rebirth and subsequent doubt is sharply aligned with abandonment by the stars in this poem written in 2020. The memory of the horrific violence is ever-present in the poem.

In "Well, my dead living" the poet writes:

"You killed the bird that used to sing in the morning, sleep now! even the dead sleep...
two meters under the dirt, under the cypress trees, no one disturbs their peace...

well, my dead living, you are free now,
no one calls you and no one awaits you,
other than at the bars and the tables
where life has been sitting, cloyed for a long time..."

There is an inherent mystery that unravels: "in what kind of bed of lies are you going to lay down alone, / when one by one from you, they'll go?" The bird could be love or life. The ambiguity creates mingled impressions, yet the imagery remains sharp and astute.

This astuteness characterizes each poem. *Golden Armor* is poetry that protests and promises refuge. The poet does not balk at world affairs. The lost, lonely soul is her concern. Like Pallas Athena from Zeus's forehead, these poems are born from the head of the poet Armenida Qyqja bearing the armor of dignity and strength.

Each poem bears an unfathomable sense of distress and longing. Natural sensuality is mingled with political fatalism:

"under the light of a lemony moon
the soul will check secretly
fate's mark on the shoulder:
a refugee's life"
("Refugee's life")

The contrast between natural images ("lemony moon") and the longings of a refugee provide the reader with hope amidst the pains and hopelessness of a refugee. The reader can truly bite into the senses of loneliness and fear these images invoke. A refugee's life is one of abandonment by the powers of the world; however, can the night sky provide solace? In these poems the reader experiences a deeper humanity. The rage of discontentedness and the pangs of longing are merged with love and honor.

8

Inside my heart

Undone is my bed, a mess,
just like my days and nights without you,
let it be! I don't want to disturb the dreams,
that wide awake, await you…

in a corner, cold feet huddle,
you know, the wait can't warm them,
in the messy sheets, pain surrenders,
turned into a fist, in a timeless time…

how many days since our last kiss?
how many nights we do not meet in my dreams,
this starless sky, tells of my longingness,
deep in my heart, to keep looking for you…

(April 2023)

Bitter thoughts

We are very lucky, my love,
very lucky to not be born in Syria,
they burned it to the ground…

and not in Iran either,
love is forbidden in that country,
how would I meet you there?

and not in Moscow, or Ukraine,
bombed are the mornings there,
the best time to make love…

we were born in a little country
that is getting emptied and refilled,
with people like us, exiled…

oh, what bitter thoughts!
take me, my love,
it's better to forget everything…

(July 2023)

Suppressed childhoods

Barefoot I go, on my tiptoes,
on the roads laid on your forehead,
searching for your childhood,
before it was forced into premature manhood,
by the desperate crowds,
the anonymous bullets,
the bodies returned by the sea's full belly…

fields and dusty roads
greet me and your eyes,
the same as now…
no one knows why I used to tiptoe,
come closer, lend me your ear,
let my hidden suppressed child
share the secret with yours…

(July 2023)

Undated battles

Stuck, impossible to process in the remains of brain's mill
the news chronicles of a gloomy Autumn,
torn words by the bombs in Gaza,
syllables that fight and cry among themselves,
over infants' bodies, mothers' wails…

we walk, drink coffee, exchange conversation,
from Europe to the middle-east,
I behold you in my eyes, my love,
there can't be a third big war I tell myself again
there, deep inside the swollen retinas…

(October 2023)

The sons and daughters of pragmatism

We, the sons and daughters of pragmatism,
wink an eye at our own image in the mirror and run along,
all alone we keep running,
life's path isn't the alley of our childhood,
that though narrow, included all our friends…

with welded hearts we run,
with rings inside our arteries, one, two, three,
as if all the time and chances
to come back from death
were ours and limitless…

my Lord, blow me out like a candle
when my time comes,
you know, I'm uncorrectable,
my foot is always on the gas pedal,
five hundred and thirty kilometers per hour,
until the tired pedal breaks
and time with it too…

(August 2024)

Mercenaries of chaos

Spiritual and mental anorexia,
that has no cure, no stimulus,
the most evil chronic condition
is going to wipe out the human race
at a much higher rate
— than all viruses created in labs…

and you, mercenaries of chaos,
what will you say one day?
to the empty skulls of your children
that won't know anything else
other than shaking involuntarily, uncontrollably,
Tequila, tequila va, va.[1]

.

(September 2024)

---

[1] "Tequila, tequila va, va" is a hit song in Albania, of no meaning
other than tequila, of uneducated "artist" generation.

Endlessly

Loneliness spreads her arms out through the night,
dancing proudly by herself,
she invites me and even changes the roles,
bowing elegantly, like a real gentleman…

but, I've made up my mind, darling,
a wallflower I shall remain, until you come,
with my eyes pinned to the wall in front of me,
where memories project our dancing shadows…

and just like that, slowly, I fall asleep
with my arms around your neck,
one, two, three, one, two, three — endlessly,
with yours wrapped around my waist…

(September 2024)

Mental paralysis

Mental paralysis camouflaged
by the buzzing of the wasps in hives,
free thought has been dead for a long time,
and now you can't even mourn it...

long live Facebook and Instagram
where we get and share wise quotes,
big brother thinks for us
and even knows our business in the bathroom...

(August 2024)

Waiting…

Muddy riverbed
and drowned thoughts in its bottom,
that imagination and patience
can't help me save today...

beyond the horizon I make way,
following the sun
on his way to you,
but you're still sleeping and I drown again,
sweetly, this time,
waiting for you to awake...

(August 2024)

Now that I have you

I cleaned my closet from all toxic things,
the dresses worn on dreadful days,
the shoes with high heels eaten from the paths of loneliness
won't crack loudly in my memory, anymore…

I threw them all out, together with the scale,
that never loved me, not even a single gram,
I can't decide what to do about the mirror,
the hell with it too, I have your eyes.

(July 2024)

Sunset of longingness

I despair when I think
that my wave of thoughts can't reach you,
you don't know how hateful the wait becomes,
in a deaf-muted space…

then, I turn to faith and love,
to your thousand kisses,
smiling, as I walk down the streets,
what a happy woman! people say…

no one knows how scorched is the heart
when sun sets with the longingness of an entire day
gathered on its chest
how I miss the soft cry of your eyes…

(July 2024)

When you shall arrive

It's known, the crows eat
everything that is sick or dead,
creatures that can't stand up to them,
black inside and out, God made them!

let them eat, let them feel satiated,
with everything that is wrong in me,
blown up let them show their pride to the sky,
beating their chests, *krraaa, krraaa, krraaa,…*

when they'll have nibbled all my weaknesses,
you shall arrive, my love,
as never before, your hands and lips
will blossom my soul…

(June 2024)

On the wet windows

We talk, the uproar of cracking skies over there
joins the noise of bad phone lines,
I hear the buzz of people that don't know what they want,
they hate the heat and complain about the rain…

the flooded streets are out there,
together with *pied-à-terre* buildings and washed-out colors,
a disgraceful make-up of prostitutes and oligarchs,
the trash cans too heavy for the flowing water…

you talk to me softly
and everything fades away,
everything but the moan of distance, all over
the wet windows of my soul,
your eyes keep writing *I miss you.*

(June 2023)

Murdered thoughts…

In your absence
thoughts crucify each other
without nails or hammers,
come my love, before they all get killed…

they blame each other endlessly,
under the fog of waiting,
tired, they fall down at the feet of the cross,
not knowing what to do with their longing for you…

do you hear the loud rappelling of the sky?
the last thought fell, another martyr,
come now and perform the miracle of resurrection!
what is a head for with no dreams needed?!

(May 2023)

Waiting to hear your voice

Somewhere, in the wait, thoughts get stuck,
reminding me of the stain of ink,
as it spreads on the parchments of time…
what happened to your voice, love,
the sky grew dark, it has become a big black stain…

I only write what my heart dictates,
from inside your heart,
and beyond them there is nothing else,
just empty endless space…

speak my love, whisper!
in a thousand words,
I'm waiting to translate that single word,
beyond which — nothing has ever existed…
I love you!

(January 2024)

Snails

Snails, always looking forward to rain,
with their carapace on their backs, feverish,
up and down they start
their crawl, slimier each time…

I don't know what I hate the most:
the crawl, the slime on the ground
or their happiness caused by the sky breakers, rain…

other creatures join from the dirt,
reminding me all of a sudden
that there are even worse things than snails,
their crawl and disgusting slimy mucus…

rain will wash away the slime from the pathway,
while later, inside those shells,
other creatures, even smaller than the snails,
shall play hide and seek…

the sacrificed snails
will not return to catch them…

(March 2024)

Somewhere, near the heart

Surrounded by the gray smog of thoughts
you sigh, defeated,
I feel pain while leaving your chest,
puff after puff…

you don't feel me love, you don't feel me,
not even when I tuck myself where I was before,
somewhere, between the lungs,
a little to the left, near the heart…

what do oceans have to do here?
countries, borders, damn fences,
my god, how many prisons
and sufferings for the soul, have we invented?

(February 2024)

That moment

There comes always that moment,
when the heartbeat starts to drown
from the silence that falls between us,
and later from your words…

I hold my breath
to the last vibration of the air
and count slowly
the centuries of the wait within each second,
until you say it again to me…

I understand the unsatiated hunger of silence
when the rain drop falls on it,
how it tries to fill itself
with its sound in every crevice…

I realize, I shall die unsatiated
somewhere, between your lips…

(February 2024)

Escalation of thoughts

The shadows play with a beam of light,
and the half-closed blinds,
they rejoice with my carelessness,
while I get startled caught by surprise…

I wrap myself around you and remind myself
those shadows wouldn't exist
without that silver thread of light,
the tree branches, near the window…

let them play with visual illusions
and the wound-up imaginations by the wind,
nothing is greater than
light itself and the actual being…

(March 2024)

Oblivion's prelude

Deafness has fallen in the Odeon of the soul
with the exit of the last spectator —
one by one — the violins shut themselves in silence,
the lungs of cellos let go their sighs…

with invisible fingers,
memory plays on pain's harp
the oblivion's prelude — again from the start,
a teardrop falls on emptiness, another follows it,
with the iron beat of the metronome,
they step on the heart…

(April 2021)

For the strong…

This darkness shall pass,
its curtains won't be able to restrain the sun forever,
close your eyes and see with the light
that you have inside your heart…

with each hour of darkness
let love grow within your breath,
with invisible lips, let it kiss your pain,
remember fate challenges only the strong ones…

lying in bed, in each other's arms,
we shall tell stories to the stars, each night,
we shall be the heroes
that rise again, from the rubble…

(February 2023)

They say….

I've been hiding from myself for a long time,
I hide from that emptiness that can't be seen in a mirror,
who in the hell, put the heart on scale?
how do they know the soul is split in two equal parts?

there is very little left of me
and so much space within each breath,
the empty beds of the capillaries,
say that you would have to move in entirely, inside me…

(February 2024)

Some peace…

The hammers beat day and night,
time's prison cell — still narrow, remains
with walls that don't give in,
how many Athenas try to beat them down
with their bloody fists?

prisons of hijabs and dogmas,
Zeuses that even two thousand years after Christ,
fear losing power...
even he couldn't teach the world about love...

the hammers beat day and night, time's
prison cell still narrow...
take me my love, take me!
I'm so tired of this raging war…

(September 2023)

They killed Mahsa

You look at me, as always full of pleasure,
while today I look at you secretly,
even though it's useless, I keep trying
to hide my thoughts to you and the mirror…

my lips are done, I'll comb my hair now
and you as usual will get up,
you will not resist, you'll cling to me,
while kissing my neck and soft curls…

something is going to break inside me darling,
and I won't be able to conceal the loud crack,
there, far away in Iran, they killed Mahsa,
just for a lock of hair, like mine…

(September 2022)

A drop of joy at the bottom of the glass

I laugh at the open black umbrellas,
while the sun is at its highest peak,
the faces that fear it,
just as much as they fear a carefree smile
over the hills of Botox…

I almost blush, as I think
that my thoughts can be read
on my eyes that are glass transparence,
hell, well, I know they laugh at me too…

of course, they laugh at my long list
of abstinences, the black coffees
and the trails of sweat
I leave behind in the gym…

an alcohol lover, at the end of the bar,
gives me a sly wink and laughs
at us, the philosophers and crazy poets,
trying to climb the ladder of imaginary success…

for him life is a drop of joy
left at the bottom of the glass,
and a very simple song,
written by a couplet songwriter,
nothing extraordinary…

(July 2024)

Heart's filters

The lens of eyes focuses
on my tired image
and the filters start their job,
to convey to your heart
my very best version…

thousands of flashes go on, nonstop,
until all the contrasts and shades
get processed one by one,
from all possible angles…

I remember to breathe,
the skin relaxes from iron tension,
thoughts, wrinkles and their waves are at rest…
it's done you say, as you take me
deeper and deeper into your heart…

(January 2024)

Digital times

Never has it been any easier
for the Devil, to buy the man,
he doesn't need gold, or paper,
just imaginary money…

millions and billions and still hungry
the Devil himself, he envies,
ready to trade everything
just to have the power, passed on to him…

the Devil doesn't mind, keeps playing his tricks,
raising him while wiping him out,
his servants are all the glorious kings,
as no one seems to know the price of the soul...

(September 2023)

Two thousand years on ruined table

How many times I've joined
your last supper, uninvited,
the thirteenth, uninvited guest,
sometimes as Judas, or Peter,
how tight on my neck
hugs the rope of this world!
twelve were the gates
and high the price…

in the lightning of your eyes
I measure your pulse,
the iron bones break
inside the heart of time…
few moments set apart
honor of a man from treason,
faith from fear,
life from death…

you dine with him,
share bread and wine,
look him in the eye
and kiss him on the forehead…
my heart drowns in my throat…
do you know? do you know?
for two thousand years on the ruined table,
the question keeps searching for the answer…

(August 2023)

Find me

I keep looking for you in the fog
that wraps around my heart,
silent, choking anxiety,
that hides heart's footprints, from eyes,
so everything gets lost with the roads...

I'm cold, freezing cold,
without your arm, your strong shoulder...
comes a moment when you feel fragile
and the Devil picks the time
to test out your friends...

like the last Autumn leaf
you tremble from the slightest breeze,
where can you hold on? where?
all lines are busy — all are busy,
each in their own whirlpool...

find me love and hold me tight,
a hug I need,
a hug that can melt the clouds around,
bring back the sun to my heart...

(May 2023)

In love…

With gentle steps you enter my heart,
releasing my torn dreams,
from the hidden trenches of the night…

oh, these dreams of mine,
how come, they never wander
around sunny paths, not even in sleep?

calmness, finally calmness,
your voice warms my bed,
seducing the sun without a rush…

I love the morning dreams
and you while becoming one
with the light, under my eyelids…

(April 2023)

It isn't late…

The clock never tells the truth,
for it can't measure correctly
the time that passes between beats
in a heart full of longingness…

here, tell me how can it be measured?
the space from breath to breath,
when even the eyes can't get enough of you
they keep lightning, without shedding tears…

time — time is exactly what was,
when my heart slept peacefully next to yours,
call me! don't be afraid of chasing from my eyes
the sleep that never got begotten…

(January 2025)

Come closer

This heartbeat is the strongest bridge
in the whole universe...
any doubts about it?
don't put it to the test anymore!
I've been loving you from so far, so long...
come closer and dare to feel
the tension each beat holds
while joining the moon and the sun,
day after day, night after night,
I told you...
I've been loving you from so far, so long,
come closer beloved!

(January 2025)

Clouded soul…

I gaze at a pair of white wings
that fly in the ash-gray winter sky
the darkened clouds can't spoil their brightness,
nor their majestic greatness…

I feel tightness, inside my chest,
where unhappiness brews
and the received arrows
stir in what I don't want to be,
my polar opposite…

tell me, you pure soul,
that fly through the dark clouds, invincible,
how can one keep himself pure
when people sell you, in front of your eyes?

(January 2025)

My eyes…

My eyes are still the same — the thirsty eyes,
that used to follow the paper airplanes,
across the room of poverty…

the metal airplanes haven't managed
to carry all the dreams across the sky,
even though life had killed many of them…

look deep, in the green branches
that shoot out of the brown velvet ground of the retina,
those are the dreams that grow with you each day…

(January 2023)

Moonless night

I got lost last night
and in darkness, I fought myself,
stronger and stronger I hit all my shadows,
even the most junior ones,
the night kept eating the moon and stars,
while laughing…

in a corner of my soul
I would hear your voice,
telling me to stop,
but where were your arms to restrain me?
to hold me and bring me back to myself?

I fought a lot my love,
until you called me on the phone…

(January 2025)

Self healing

Pain bites my heart,
sparks fly from her teeth and spread in the dark,
I rejoice, it hasn't rusted,
the wait and disappointments, haven't defeated it…

inside of it, your laughter echoes,
you laugh at my stupidities,
December that drags on the frozen roads,
the icy cold, that can't freeze love…

my heart keeps beating peacefully
and with medicine of your voice
self heals itself, after each bite,
people wonder how is it possible?

(December 2024)

In every single drop

Peaceful, wintery panorama
replicated on the river's body
and clouds that walk slowly,
so to not break its serenity…

I get closer to that watery mirror
that I may leave my image on it, too,
in the memory of every single drop
I'll be glazed, even when I'm gone…

just like I am in your eyes,
the greatest crystal lakes, I've ever seen…

(January 2025)

Last six's[2] fever

The world gasps while on cataclysm
and tears blend with the sweat of agony,
that so many times, have escaped a biblical ending,
miraculously, at the last minute…

strangely, the heart beats stronger and stronger,
like flattering wings of a wild bird,
trying to escape the fatal grip of a trap,
the iron teeth, that are everywhere…

one more time, it is trying hard to escape,
but doesn't dare to call God for help,
while the forehead is burning
from the fire of the last six's fever…

(February 2024)

---

[2] The last six's… meaning the last 6 of 666 (the mark of the beast).

Untruthful words

Untruthful words
cast their eclipse over the eyes' pathway,
there shall be light again
but we won't be able to see each other like before…

silence is going to kill
what remains hostage of memory
little by little each day,
until nothing moves him anymore…

yeah, that's what's going to happen,
don't look for new paths,
or connecting bridges between us,
not after that poisoned moment
where the heart fell today…

(December 2023)

Where can I wait for you?

Your absence and time
open some small holes in me,
some visible, some invisible...

I try to stop them,
but I can't manage all by myself,
two against one,
totally unfair, I think...

even the marble statues grow old,
the wind — wet air of loneliness,
carry on the job of the invisible gnawers,
sculpting wrinkles, cracking veins...

tell me, where can I wait for you love
so that their teeth won't get me?

(December 2024)

Brighter days will come

Fate's pincer doesn't honor celebrations or holy days,
it keeps tightening its grip on the heart,
it doesn't care about the great gap between the edges,
nor about lost blood — the agony...

but the heart needs only one drop of blood, one beat,
to travel from far and reach you in a moment,
just to say *good morning, love*
as soon as you open your eyes,
like nothing ever happened...

one day, tired will be that heartless piece of metal,
of course, it will be, my love,
rusted from the blood, will surrender,
there will be brighter days, of course there will be...

(December 2023)

Let kisses write the future

The present writes our future,
but don't worry, don't think about it,
let dream's castles build themselves,
the ones we built before, got ruined by storms…

tie your fingers with mine and follow me
where the wind becomes breath on life's lips,
there where nothing exists
other than the rhythmic stroke of the heartbeat…

once, we were the world, you and I,
the first twin embryo that Eden birthed,
come, don't be afraid to return to innocence,
let the kisses, plant the future in the garden…

(July 2022)

Your love

It happens that I get delayed on my way to you,
gloomy ponds devour my steps,
the world never forgets to pour the rain of misery,
from down-up, endlessly…

with a little chunk of sun in your hands
you wait for me, patiently,
and you smile at my silhouette,
as always, from far…

never a scolding, no bitter words,
only kisses await me on your lips,
how else could it be?! I'm your love,
in a completely mad time…

(March 2024)

No use to deny it

You are mine, and only mine
with all your pluses and minuses,
that never know rest,
even in sleep, with weapons loaded…

enough trying to flee from the heart,
the cave of the soul — that's drying
each hour without you,
let go and don't fear the flood,
the rushed waterfall of the feeling…

come, as you are, a wild river,
more uncorrectable than yesterday,
mine, you are mine — mine only,
no use to deny it, useless to flee, run away…

(February 2022)

On the roads of my soul

Still snowing here,
I guess I still need to learn
how to walk with small steps,
slow down and read the reactions around...

life is a great teacher,
but love is even greater,
patiently, teaching me how to have faith,
even when all roads are frozen...

the meteorologists promise it will be followed by...
who listens to their promises anymore?
I hear your breathing as you rush
to warm up the roads of my soul...

(January 2025)

Time for love

Winter arrived here, without even a knock,
didn't give Autumn a chance to enjoy its days,
I don't feel for her as much as I feel for those birds,
left out there, hostage to the nest they couldn't leave behind…

six degrees Celsius and rain,
shivering in the sleepy morning,
but don't worry my love,
your smile I'm wearing…

I hear the fluttering wings of the butterflies
of those sunwarm days, beside you,
the sweet rustle, inside my heart I feel,
just like then, with each touch and kiss…

but do you hear that? the sky is emptying,
the vapor of longingness and the ropes of rain
have layered the windows inside and out,
come, it's time for love…

(October 2022)

How far

I keep counting the days, hours, the breaths away from you,
while the world keeps going the same way, same habits,
from stones, to spears, nuclear missiles,
the gravediggers are building bunkers, again...

with open eyes I dream of you and I,
laying on a green valley, under the sun,
I don't hear the news or the axes anymore,
nor the hysterical tick of the atomic clock...

how many more breaths
are you away from me love?
it's the only thing I really want to know,
this numb January morning...

(January 2024)

Freely…

Freely inside and out of your lungs
that eagerly await me,
calculating my absence
to the hundredth part of the second…

what more would a woman need?
to feel beautiful,
a powerful Cleopatra,
in her own reign!

on their echoing chords I place my head,
and I listen to the music of air,
on the peaceful soul,
dome after dome…
behind I would leave all the kingdoms, for it…

do you know love?
the most beautiful symphonies
are those that could never be written…

(June 2023)

I hear

I hear the beating of hearts,
together with the whisper of the fluttering wings,
at the moment they join the sky…

I keep hearing them,
even when lose my sight,
I just have to keep silent…

love is a free bird
and I'm thankful it exists
even when I'm left alone…

we'll be together soon, very soon,
every bit of air, tells me,
while carrying your heartbeat
full of love, to me…

(June 2024)

Always

I look at myself in the mirror
and talk to your image,
stamped in the retina of my eyes…

I tell him many things,
and I notice that solitude has added
a couple of new grey strands to my hair…

the heart keeps repeating your words
about pointless worries
and the Summer's sun dresses my face…

what about time, my love?
will time know us
the same way we'll always know each other?

(January 2024)

There's no surrender

I'm left alone with just my fallen knights
and my cries, trying to get them to rise again,
telling them, there's no surrender,
because a heart is waiting for me out there,
beyond the ambushes, in fear's forest…

I tell them, to get over their tired selves,
because beyond the suffocating vacuum of loss,
there's a breath, holding itself breathlessly,
while waiting for me,
to find my way between those two lips…

there's no surrender, because I have two strong arms,
that keep the chest open in the midst of Winter, for me,
there isn't, nor could ever be, surrender now,
with love so nearby, finally!

(January 2023)

The only thing I need

I pray for the bread of the soul,
while death brings the bargains higher,
sending inflation beyond the stratosphere,
trying to colonize space…

I'm neither blind nor deaf,
I know where disaster will make its fatal landing,
but I can't care less, for anything worldly,
love is enough for my ark…

sleep in peace! burning are the candles
and I'm just where I should be, near you…

(November 2023)

The dawn of my day

Night's heavy breathing, can be heard in the sky,
its tired run, full of anguish,
shivering from cold and fear,
scared of its own shadows on the walls of reason...

the heart talks softly to her and the reason,
holding her hand in hers,
so that she may not fear the dark,
the long hardship, your absence...

the night runs and runs, my love,
without a rest, a breath,
stretching out her steps to reach the light,
the light inside your eyes...

(August 2023)

About love, again…

I wrote about you, again,
even though, there's thousands of things
that I should write about…

I'm not alone,
that's what a whole world of displaced people does,
it wraps itself in its own shell,
pretending to forget its problems, illnesses,
the autistic children that grow in numbers, each day…

forgets the debts
and through blasting sirens, even death…
no one counts the days of war
there, in that place that once was Ukraine

some places get emptied with bombs and fires,
some other places, like mine,
with the colorless gas of poisoned hope…
a homeless world and me…
a Joseph sold by my own brothers, so cheap…

thousands of things I should write about,
I should, I know very well, I must!
but here we are!
I wrote about you, again…

(September 2023)

Confession

The first escape happened as soon as I woke up,
did you feel me on your chest, my love?
the shouts of the alarm clock ordered my body to work
while the body cried for you like a wounded animal…

the second escape, happened sometime late morning,
the news in the background kept talking about the new order,
the endless war in Ukraine,
while my colleagues chattered about lots of stuff,
an Apple watch among them…

should I go on?
we haven't even arrived at lunch,
the background news
about the new asylum seekers
in England,
the corrupt FBI,
the praises and gossip of my colleagues…

I've escaped so many times,
all the times only with you,
did you hear my crazy heartbeat
as it jumped one by one, the meridians?
far away, I took you with me,
far from everything and everyone,
they've all gone crazy since a long time ago,
they don't know what they want,
while I want only, for you to love me…

(April 2023)

The asylum seekers… still a lot of illegal immigrants risking their
lives with boats to immigrate to England.
The corrupt FBI: McGonigal skandal in ties with Albanian mp.

360 degrees

Thoughts spin at 360 degrees
and return again to the origin,
where else can they go?
when you are me
and I am you, in every single point…

I'm back my love, I'm back,
with a greater longing for you than before,
with my heart in my hands, I praised the axis
that a whole universe keeps on its feet,
for me, only…

(May 2024)

Well, my dead living…

You killed the bird that used to sing in the morning,
sleep now! even the dead sleep…
two meters under the dirt, under the cypress trees,
no one disturbs their peace…

well, my dead living, you are free now,
no one calls you and no one awaits you,
other than at the bars and the tables
where life has been sitting, cloyed for a long time…

the circle will get narrower one day,
boys grow old and the girls don't taste like before,
in what kind of bed of lies are you going to lay down alone,
when one by one from you, they'll go?

(March 2022)

In every single bit

In my veins, sadness flows secretly,
eyes and lips struggle to defeat it, at all cost!
thoughts race the light
to bring you here, next to my heart…

there's only air, air,
just empty space between us,
let them measure it however they like,
in every single bit of longingness, you're mine…

I mastered all my vocal chords,
not to let my voice betray Summer,
here from my end, no clouds, no rain,
just a fall, steeper and steeper, deep in my heart…

(August 2023)

By the shore of the light

Patience, my dear, patience,
God is aware how much air is left in our lungs,
at the right moment, he will bring us out,
just like Joan, by the shore of light…

the long wait and anxiety are not going to grind us down,
nor the sharp teeth of distress,
precalculated is everything,
to the millimetric fragments of time…

we had to pass through this dark path,
in order to better know ourselves and others,
to also know what love can do,
when planted by God's hands in the heart…

(September 2023)

Such yearning...

You don't know the taste of the mornings,
nor that of the dinners, or evenings,
the taste of dew that lands on my soul,
when you talk to me, with your eyes only...

one doesn't live on bread alone,
we both know it very well,
the hunger of the soul can't be filled by a spoon,
nor with lies they tell us, without a flinch in the eye...

I close my eyes and I see you again,
even bigger, inside of me,
you don't know the taste of days,
that wake up with such yearning for you...

(August 2022)

Unsatiated thoughts

A bunch of flies rush to get full
on the waste left on the dinner table,
such great appetites for such small bellies,
isn't that always?

in a million directions we rush, unsatiated,
forgetting the small cycle,
the trap of the short circuit of time,
that we'll take nothing with us when we die…

the noise of the express doesn't move the flies,
not the thoughts that buzz unsatiated,
without even knowing their own yearning,
shamelessly, more and more wanting…

take me away from the table, the flies' dinner party,
the thoughts that unsatiated will remain till they'll die,
I know, behind our backs there will be such gossip,
but won't people do that anyway?

(January 2023)

Refugee's life

The day bites its lips until they bleed,
with a child's eye
and a woman's heart, kept waiting for you
but you didn't come, you couldn't…
a deaf night shall fall on her,
muted again,
with the voice of longing tight around the throat…
under the light of a lemony moon
the soul will check secretly
fate's mark on the shoulder:
a refugee's life
the walls of flesh will feel the red iron,
the burning agony of hell while alive…
pain will shut the jaws tight,
to drown its cries,
that's how they have branded cattle for centuries…

(January 2023)

There, far away…

The moon can't wait any longer!
all swollen like a woman in her last hours of labor,
it has come out in the middle of the sky,
to wait for the night, but the day doesn't care,
it's still her time…

with my hands, I hold down all my voices,
the impatience that wants to come to you,
but you, have you managed to hold tight
the blood in your veins?

I don't know why, I feel like
I'm drowning in the moon's wild river
and in the gurgle of your blood
that rushes out there, far away…

(January 2025)

Roses in the snow

Have you ever seen the roses
that bloom in the middle of the snow?
love that challenges Winter,
the frozen frames of time…

wind blows like crazy
snow, snow! shout out all weathermen,
with their cold voices,
from icy January's hall ends…

come, kiss my eyes
in lush pink petals, let's cover the snow,
what a pity for the blind,
that can't see their beauty…

(January 2023)

Bargain noises

The virus keeps competing with Hydra,
in peace, no one is out there to kill it anymore,
the face masks, got dumped in trash cans,
anti-vaccines soar in the market…

amphibian people, plastic, alien, microchip,
what a crazy bargain noise,
all kinds of stupidities to numb mankind,
from America all the way to Ukraine…

666 heads, with no race or gender,
all over the world, day and night, make fun of prophecies,
what kind of experiment will be next in line?
the empty tv screen oracles, are asking Soros….

(July 2023)

Human

We never talk about our wound,
but silently drink the pain from each other's eyes,
without a single word, we place our lips,
where the world accidently
keeps tearing the crust on the wound …

we never talk about the past, the bloody duels,
we don't ask for mercy, or medals,
fans of the present thirsty for life,
we know how to smile through pain…

the hell with empty talks, word's elevator,
the hands that try to probe our wounds,
if two thousand times more, they'd put Christ to die
nothing would change, simply, human race…

(September 2022)

The miracle...

Some wounds can never be healed,
what can time do, my love,
when inside the lungs, even air aches,
just from the whispers in our mind...

one can learn to live,
like the tree with a bad trim from gardeners,
it fights to grow new shoots,
so that birds can build nests on its branches...

do you hear this crazy beat
that from the chest keeps throwing the heart?
come, wildly, breath on me,
heartaches make the hunger for life grow bigger...

(February 2023)

Without your voice

Tied up are my hands and thoughts,
turned into knots without your voice,
in the trap of a muted wait
falls time, unable to breathe any more…

let those measuring devices say what they want,
I was never good at figuring them out,
all the way to the bottom, I lowered the inner voices,
that scold me down for wasting my time…

wanting, always more wanting,
something, all the time, endlessly,
but without your voice — heart's engines can't run,
words of love they need, to make light…

(August 2023)

Calm

I've let time carry on with its own business
of counting the grains of sand,
she knows there's nothing she can do about me…

my pyramid can't be consumed
by the whips of wind — nor the shifting poles
so feverishly talked about…

she continues her ritual, anyway,
the endless counting
from earth's skin, calling out magma,
with each grain that falls from her hands…

like a calm Dea,[3] I laugh,
my pyramid is safe,
inside your heart,
what could I possibly fear in there?

(April 2024)

---

[3] *Dea- goddess of beauty*

Pilgrimage of the soul

Along deceiving landscapes of life, we journey,
deceiving forests, valleys, oases,
just as the soul's lips get ready for a sip,
rivers change their flow, unquenched thirst
remains…

we keep on walking, unfollowed by our own ideals
and so many friends we used to love,
with ease, they stroll through well-leveled grounds,
wider paths and tamed climate…

thinned are the soles of shoes,
tired, the feet from the endless hills,
on your own shadow, lean on, man,
if faithful you've been to yourself, all the way…

(October 2023)

The most beautiful motive

Coffee continues its mission
of raising the blood pressure,
as it drags around without desire,
in the sleepless rooms of memories…

eyes closed it remains in bed and thinks about you,
while conscience and your voice tell him to move,
go get on with the journey,
complete the chores, the unfinished businesses…

I'll gather myself and get going,
the grains of wheat at the top of the pyramid,
look at you and me,
when together we shall be one, one day…

(July 2024)

Just listen

Your lips find my thoughts,
traversing half of the earth,
in the time that the heart needs
— from beat to beat…

let a scientist put their stopwatch on it,
let them measure the speed of the waves,
that hold the circuit between two hearts…
— I'm too busy for that…

I love you my love, a lot, endlessly,
let me say all the things you can't say,
you just listen with your eyes closed and never forget,
the most beautiful axiom of the universe
— is love…

(September 2023)

Your fingers tell me…

Innocence keeps shaking painfully,
along with small parts of my body,
a shoulder, almost isn't there anymore,
nor the eye that kept seeking goodness
in the endless mourning…

we have gotten used, since long ago,
with the silent abandonments,
turned backs during dark hours,
and still, we keep getting more
and more fresh new cracks on our souls…

you caress me softly, quietly,
like a happy archeologist,
with the remaining pieces of a mosaic…

your fingers tell me
you would never exchange me,
not even with a perfect, whole art piece…

(January 2024)

Heart's coordinates do not change

The sky on this end, misses a handful of stars,
smog and clouds cover passionately their burning sparks,
in the second floor, a dreamless sleep,
sleeps my bed…

I start out without a light or fire,
like the blinds I count the steps in space,
the empty breaths,
from one edge of loneliness to your lips…

the soul knows the way, even with his eyes closed,
let them spin him around until dizziness,
old game of ignorant children,
the coordinates of the heart never change…

(August 2023)

Simply, woman

You came just in time, when you were most needed,
behind the curtains, tired were the prayers,
let the strong woman have a rest now,
in your arms, to bed carry me tonight!

to strong people — the world belongs, always,
but I'm laying my weapons down tonight,
giving you the chance to be strong for me,
while I take a nap, on your cozy chest…

in old tales let the amazons battle,
invincible and glorious as ever,
I've fought so much I don't miss the swords,
the flashings of the soul on their sharp edges…

simply a woman, I'd like to be now,
come darling, do spoil me, finally!

(November 2022)

Emotion

You are the emotion that awakens my hours,
caught breathless, under the sand dunes,
in the deserts I walked, half of my lifetime,
with the faith, that my steps betrayed…

I found you and myself suddenly,
the shadow that ventured, unknowingly,
like a Hebrew in the promised land,
my heart felt, inside yours…

you are the emotion, the time and the beat,
the vibe that trembles, immeasurably,
in vain I keep trying to put you in my verses,
words could never weave your Psalms…

(June 2023)

To my companion

I'm where the paths of the heart, grow narrower,
step after step, I talk to your breath,
to hold on and not give up,
to the light of your eyes, I say: *get up!*
together we shall pass this dark path

that's life sometimes you, sometimes me,
tired, at the bottom of the slope, defeated,
give me your lips and I'll give you back,
the air, the breath that once grew my days,
reaching for the sun, hungrily…

how else would you know,
that I really love you?

(October 2023)

Praying for peace

So this is the white heron,
my childhood nickname…
there it is, combing its snow-white feathers,
in the lagoon's heart, calmly…

a peaceful moment and this beautiful bird!
but how would it be when the wind enrages
the waves and the predators rush
to snatch the prey from each other's beaks?

The law of survival ruins the picture
and makes me pray for peace…

(Nov 2024)

With you in my heart

They keep talking about the end, on and on,
so sure about its coming,
the signs, the prophecies, endless accusations,
and still ready for war, everyone ready...

covered in battle smoke they talk about the end,
the true horror, the Armageddon,
while I think about you and for the first time
feel my lungs satiate with air...

they talk and eagerly dig out the end
but I don't want to hear them any longer,
hungry for life more than ever
I chose to believe in heart's power...

(Dec 2023)

Behind the makeup

Behind the makeup hide the sleepless agonies,
self-judgments and the torturing question:
how to get by another day without you,
I don't even want to think beyond twenty-four hours…

birds without souls wait outside in a row,
ready to carry me far away,
to places where clouds and fog hang
for days and weeks,
where I'll have to find my way
like blind people do, orienting myself
by chasing the sound of your voice,
to know what time it is,
when I should wake up,
what should I do…

that's how I'll get dressed, put on my makeup
and continue to hide from the world
the thousand things it can't grasp,
thank God for the colors
and you, who lighten up my eyes,
even from far distances…

(Dec 2024)

Wonderful mess

You have fallen in love with me
and all my mistakes,
the wonderful mess,
the strong beliefs, the doubts,
the voices inside me that keep
changing personas,
anytime I get under your skin,
it's not enough to walk in your shoes only…

you could have fallen in love with
the perfect woman, who measures
even the weight of the air between words,
who doesn't err and never falls,
a woman who is never seen
without her hair and face made up,
not even in bed!

but you know why Olympus was abandoned,
not even the gods could resist temptation!
this wonderful mess,
this shattered soul with one thousand cracks,
knows how to love you without fearing the broken…

(Apr 2024)

Around the heart

Softly, I pull the thread of your thoughts
and wrap it around my heart,
still letting it free,
like a kite in the blue sky…

don't worry love,
the heart knows how to feel the wind's pulse,
how much to pull, how much to let go,
when the first drops of rain will appear…

fly my love, fly,
I've got you wrapped, safely around my heart…

(Dec 2024)

For myself and you

I'm running away, to a cave of loneliness.
in search of myself,
you know how to find me and all the passwords,
that open the paths…

when you'll come
and smell my hair lovingly,
it will be just the fragrance,
no smell of the crowds, no mishmashed thoughts…

I'm going now, I'm leaving,
so that I can give you again
the woman you love and only that one!
just give me some time,
to undress them all from myself…

(July 2024)

Kosovo[4]

I know that you shed tears inside your heart,
even when you smile,
the eyes that try to hide them in their corners, tell me,
the wet voice that trembles in the air...
how can you rejoice the day
when at night you count the years
without your child...
from the common grave a hand reaches out
to wipe out your tears, Kosovo...
your returned soul, century after century
doesn't know why it is reborn,
drenched in blood again and again to die...
we've come back to a more miserable time, will it be the last?
you kiss the hand and gently cover it with dirt again,
through tears, you try to smile at the day,
but the stars once more have abandoned your sky...

(Jan 2020)

---

[4] *This poem is dedicated to Kosovo's genocide in 1999. More than 1100 children were killed and disappeared. Thousands of bodies were buried in massive graves. 9000 people died. A repeated genocide.*

Lack of freedom

You play with a strand of my hair
fallen from my shoulders,
the mountain ridges on your forehead move,
hunched over landscapes created by the question
that rises and falls, endlessly:
in how many tragic chapters can be written
the tragic fate of our seed?
where to start and where to end?

this place, doesn't like kisses
nor men who drown in the eyes of a woman…
since impossible it is to hold me in your arms,
you keep playing with the strand of hair,
surrendered softly to your fingers…

(Nov 2024)

Arms that hold the universe

Love, the only thing that makes sense
in all the mess, thousands of pieces that fight,
but still can't find their places,
not everything broken can be glued back again...

restless movement,
in the effort to organize chaos,
and you, you never get upset
when I have to start from scratch
after the fall, over and over again...

movement, organization, reorganization,
a universe that tries to have order
each time a dream falls into an abyss...
what would I ever do without your arms!

(Nov 2023)

Mothers...

By the burning fire, winter will warm,
cozy, will unwind itself to sleep,
cold is going to keep me awake all night,
my mother's shiver, up there, in the clouds...

uncovered remain one of her shoulders,
that handful of dirt I couldn't throw!
although, frost will drip on it bitterly,
her blessings she will give me, lovingly...

her hand will stretch out, to cover me, like always,
when life shall pull its covers away from me,
to God she will pray, my sins to be forgiven,
just like all mothers, forever, effortlessly...

(Nov 2022)

Not for us…

Don't be afraid, let autumn's wind blow madly,
our love doesn't live in deciduous trees,
let the roads be covered with the fallen promises of a season
that could hold onto its own branches…

don't be afraid, the seasons aren't for us,
their comings and goings,
with the inflated suitcases of whims,
our love doesn't live in them,
let autumn take all of them with her…

let night steal the day out each second,
our love doesn't live anywhere,
but inside the sparks of our heartbeats,
let the days get smaller under winter's shadow…

don't be afraid my love, seasons aren't for us…

(Oct 2022)

Fatal combination

Enough to see you lost in me,
that's all it takes for my heart
to warm up and get drunk in love,
the glass is just part of the evening decor,
and the red wine, a background color…

who needs alcohol on a night like this?
I get drunk just on the air where your breath wanders,
useless to try to hide the loud drum of my heart,
that feels like it's going to burst with each beat…

you may finish my glass too if you like,
I'm drunk enough for days and weeks already…
what a fatal combination
this gaze and the lost words on your lips…

(September 2022)

Longing for the distant past...

Betrayed summer, again,
from rains that never cease,
under the fake morning, the clouds rejoice,
once more, their victory...

I feel such longing for the hot days
the heat wave that burns the Mediterranean's breasts,
the filtered light, on the grape vine,
sneaking in from the window,
through the heavy chintz curtains...

in a day like this, you should know my dear,
great longing I have for the distant past,
a whole chapter is missing from my genesis,
before the apple and the migration to the big world...

(July 2024)

South wind

My sighs set the south wind on fire,
the palm trees by the sea, wander in surprise,
from one hill to another, olive trees ask November
from where did he bring the heat?

unknown I walk, among people,
anonymous guilt – responsible, unrepentant,
the south wind takes her revenge, messing my hair,
you are not here to hold away her hands…

(Nov 2024)

Simple

The brain fights continuously social media's amoebas
trying to recognize itself each morning,
the eyes that know me beyond the skin,
remind to love myself, as I am...

I finished my makeup, simple, as usual,
couple of lines and some red lipstick,
no reason to worry, what more do I need,
when the light of those eyes shines on me...

(Jun 2024)

When mirrors talk

The art of lying, we master each day,
to the point, we forget and deceive ourselves,
the cured image in the mirror has no mouth to talk,
in our faces, can't throw the truth…

but, a fragile moment comes,
when you hush and all mirrors speak out,
even those of the ponds, and trust me,
after long, miserable rains,
nothing beautiful they have to say…

(July 2023)

Few droplets of joy

The news of war, has numbed our brains,
here in the West, we changed the channel,
to Christmas carols we listen now
and meteorologists' prophecies…

while, small worlds drown in misery
in the cacophony of the media,
global hypnosis and smoke of flambeaus,
inside the buildings, where parliament sections fail…

I switched the channel, too,
and lost myself in the clouds of my soul,
this December day,
for the eyes that I love for love more than the sun,
tell me, where can I find a few droplets of joy…

(Dec 2023)

For my soul's sake

Sunday!
I'm going to declare it amnesty day,
not because I truly forgive
those who hurt my soul,
but because I need a day to rest…

only one day,
to heal my heart, a little,
it's eaten walls,
dark thoughts are such horrible rodents!

I'll set them free from their prison
for one day only,
fully aware, they'll do wrong again,
in the first given opportunity,
they'll put themselves back, in their place…

oh, but, It's Sunday today!
amnesty day I shall declare,
for my soul's sake, not theirs…

(Nov 2024)

From the abandoned bay

Not even a sound, a whisper,
the elegant herons are gone,
the abandoned bay doesn't know
what to say, without them here…

silent are the ancient waters,
the cobblestone streets under them,
their girls turned into nymphs
and men have tried to catch them
in their nets, since then…

we'll have time my love,
many days and nights,
I'll tell you about the city lying under water,
the beautiful nymphs
and how unnecessary are the nets…

(Nov 2024)

Armenida Qyqja was born in Tirana, Albania in 1977 and immigrated to Canada in 1995. She is the author of eight poetry books and two books of short stories:

"Beyond the rails of rain", poetry (Dec 2018)
"Letters without envelopes", poetry (Sep 2010)
"Between the heart beats", poetry (Sep 2020)
"Kisses in ether" poetry, poetry (Sep 2020)
"Forty plus", poetry (Nov 2021)
"A bunch of poems instead of flowers",
collection of poems, (Aug 2022)
"The laughing dead", short stories (Nov 2022)
"Sizif of my soul", poetry (Feb 2023)
"Return the heart to spring", poetry (Feb 2023)
"Upon the half head of a bunker", poetry (Apr 2024)
"Ash piles"

Contents

SCAN TO VISIT AUTHOR WEBSITE

www.ingramcontent.com/pod-product-compliance
Lightning Source LLC
LaVergne TN
LVHW051603080426
835510LV00020B/3108